Tom McGowen

AIR RAID!

BOMBING CAMPAIGNS
OF WORLD WAR II

TWENTY-FIRST CENTURY BOOKS
Brookfield, Connecticut

Cover photograph courtesy of Archive Photos
Photographs courtesy of Hulton Getty/Liaison Agency: pp. 4, 10, 12, 15, 22, 28, 34, 39, 44,
63; Süddeutscher Verlag-Bilderdienst: pp. 8, 9, 18, 19, 26, 37; San Diego Aerospace
Museum: pp. 20, 31, 42, 56; Brown Brothers: p. 40; Archive Photos: pp. 47, 50 (Popper-
foto), 54, 60 (American Stock), 61; Public Record Office (ref. AIR 14/3647): p. 49

Library of Congress Cataloging-in-Publication Data

McGowen, Tom.
Air raid : the bombing campaigns of World War II / Tom McGowen.
p. cm. - (Military might)
Includes bibliographical references and index.
ISBN 0-7613-1810-0 (lib. bdg.)
1. World War, 1939-1945-Aerial operations, German-Juvenile literature. 2. World
War, 1939-1945-Aerial operations, British-Juvenile literature. 3. World War,
1939-1945-Aerial operations, American-Juvenile literature. 4. Bombing, Aerial-Great
Britain-History-20th century-Juvenile literature. 5. Bombing,
Aerial-Germany-History-20th century-Juvenile literature. 6. Bombing,
Aerial-Japan-History-20th century-Juvenile literature. [1. Bombers. 2. World War,
1939-1945-Aerial operations, German-Juvenile literature. 3. World War,
1939-1945-Aerial operations, British-Juvenile literature. 4. World War,
1939-1945-Aerial operations, American-Juvenile literature. 5. Airplanes, Military.] I.
Title. II. Series.

D785 .M42 2001
940.54'4943-dc21   00-041806

Published by Twenty-First Century Books
A Division of The Millbrook Press, Inc.
2 Old New Milford Road
Brookfield, Connecticut 06804
www.millbrookpress.com

Contents

Chapter 1

THE BIRTH OF THE BOMBERS

Not long after the Wright brothers made the first successful airplane flight on December 17, 1903, most people felt sure airplanes would become a marvelous form of transportation. But hardly anyone realized they could also become something else —a *weapon* that would change the way war was fought!

Some military leaders decided that airplanes could be used in war for scouting. A pilot in a plane high in the sky could easily see enemy troop movements and bring useful information back to his army's commanders. Eventually, the armies of most major nations all had some airplanes for scouting. But no one seemed aware, yet, that an airplane could be used for attack.

In 1911, Italy and Turkey went to war. Italy had a few planes that were used for scouting, at first. But then, its pilots did something that had never been done before. They dropped grenades on Turkish troops. The bomber was born.

A passenger zeppelin flies over the British fleet. This photograph was taken in Kiel, Germany, in 1914, just before the start of World War I.

World War I began in Europe in August 1914. The armies of the main opponents—the British Empire (Britain, Canada, Australia, New Zealand, India, and a number of other nations), France, Russia, and Belgium, on one side, Germany and Austria on the other—had small forces of airplanes. Germany also had airships; huge gas-filled, lighter-than-air crafts somewhat like modern blimps, generally called "zeppelins," after their inventor. These could be driven through the air by an engine at about 60 miles (97 kilometers) an hour, or could drift silently with the engine shut off, like a balloon.

At first, each side used its airplanes only for scouting the enemy. But shortly after the beginning of the war, a German pilot flew his plane over the city of Paris and dropped four small bombs, killing one person and injuring four others. He apparently hoped to frighten the Parisians into surrendering, because he also dropped a note urging them to do so. This was the first time in history that a city was bombed by an airplane.

Bombing became more frequent and deliberate; it was ordered by commanders, rather than done at a pilot's whim. Precise targets were selected. In September, a British plane was sent to the German city of Düsseldorf to bomb a hangar containing a zeppelin. The bombs hit the hangar squarely and destroyed the airship in a fiery explosion.

Bombs at this time were fairly small and weighed only about ten pounds (4.5 kilograms). They were generally carried right beside the pilot. To drop a bomb, he simply picked one up, held it over the side of the plane, and let it go. Later, inventors in each country figured out ways of attaching bombs to the underside of a plane, and dropping them by yanking a cord or pushing a lever.

Military commanders of the nations at war began to see that bombing could be a very powerful form of warfare. They recognized that bombing could be used in two ways. One way was tactical, the other strategic.

The word "tactics" means methods used to win a battle. Aircraft bombing enemy troops, vehicles, and artillery during a battle would be doing tactical bombing. The word "strategy" means a plan to win a whole war. So strategic bombing would be a way of trying to actually destroy an enemy nation's ability to fight a war. Aircraft bombing factories that produced weapons, ammunition, and equipment, and bombing roads, railroads, and shipping facilities to prevent the flow of supplies, equipment, and troops to where they were needed would be doing strategic bombing. Of course, these kinds of targets were almost always in cities, so it was obvious that most strategic bombing would be done to cities.

The small airplanes in use in the early months of the war couldn't make long flights, such as from Germany to Britain, to do any strategic bombing. But zeppelins could. Early in 1915, Germany started a campaign of bombing British cities with zeppelins. On the night of January 19, hidden by clouds and darkness, two zeppelins floated over the English Channel, the strip of sea between Britain and France, to the port town of Great Yarmouth, on England's coast. They dropped thirty bombs that killed four people, injured sixteen, and damaged several buildings.

The people of England were shocked and terrified. A plan for defending the coast from air attacks was quickly made. Searchlights and anti-aircraft guns—cannons that could fire exploding projectiles up into the sky—were put around coastal towns. "Listening posts" were set up along the coast, and people listened there for the sound of motors in the sky.

But the Germans did not intend to bomb only coastal cities. On the night of May 31, zeppelin LZ-38 flew inland to London, capital city of the British Empire and site of Buckingham Palace, residence of the British king and queen. The city was brightly lit, not expecting attack from the sky. The LZ-38 leisurely dropped 150 bombs, damaging parts of the city and killing and injuring 42 people.

This artist's rendering depicts LZ-38 zeppelins bombing industrial buildings in an English harbor town.

Zeppelins continued to make raids on London throughout 1915. Their main targets were docks, train stations, and government buildings, but, of course, a number of private homes were destroyed, and a number of people were killed and injured. Bombs were bigger now, and some bombs dropped on London weighed 660 pounds (300 kilograms).

The British government hurriedly moved to defend London. The city was ringed with anti-aircraft guns and searchlights. Airfields were constructed nearby, and fighter planes armed with machine guns began nightly patrols over the city.

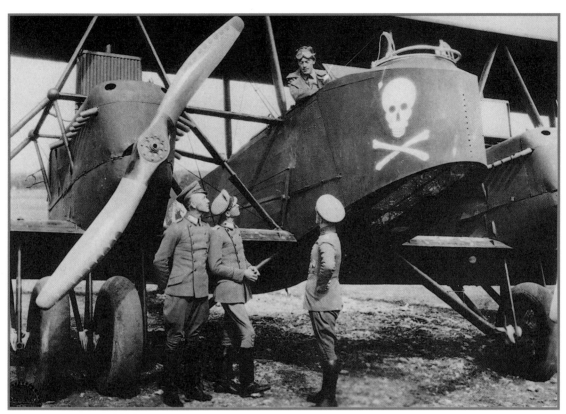

A German Gotha bomber. The rail in front of the pilot encircles another seat where a machine-gunner could sit.

During 1916, 21 zeppelins were shot down or destroyed by severe weather. The German commanders decided zeppelins were just too big, too slow, and too flimsy to be good bombers. They authorized the building of airplanes especially designed as bombers—fast, capable of carrying a heavy load of bombs a long distance, and well able to defend themselves. Like most World War I airplanes, these aircraft, known as Gothas, after the company that built them, were biplanes, with upper and lower wings. They were big planes, with 78-foot-long (24 meters) wings and two engines. They could reach a speed of 80 miles

Handey Page heavy bombers, photographed near Dunkirk, France, were the British answer to the Gotha.

(130 kilometers) an hour and fly 6 hours carrying 1,100 pounds (500 kilograms) of bombs.

The Gothas were put into a unit called Heavy Bombing Squadron Number 3. The squadron made its first raid on May 25, 1917. That Friday afternoon, people in the little seaport town of Folkestone were doing their weekend shopping. Twenty-one Gothas came from high in the sky above the sea without being seen or heard by anyone. Suddenly there were explosions. A clothing store in the center of the town collapsed, burying people within it. The railway station was damaged, and a house was destroyed. Ninety-five people were killed, 195 injured.

By autumn of 1917, the British and French also had big bombers like the Gothas. In November, British bombers taking off from airfields in France began to make strategic air raids against targets in Germany—steel factories in the city of Saarbrücken and ships in the harbor of Ludwigshaven.

During 1918, there were titanic battles as Allied and German armies struggled to gain a final, overwhelming victory. Tactical bombing was done by both Allies and Germans, as groups of 20 or 30 planes bombed bridges, railroad centers, airfields, places where supplies and ammunition were stored, and camps where troops were gathered. Strategic bombing was expanded, as German Gothas made raids on London and Paris, and British bombers struck Saarbrücken, Bonn, Wiesbaden, and other German cities.

Thus, when World War I ended in November, 1918, the use of airplanes for bombing both enemy troops and enemy cities had become a commonplace act of war.

Chapter 2

NEW IDEAS AND ANOTHER WAR

When World War I ended, military leaders of every nation began to study significant events of the war, to try to find ways of improving their army's ability to fight. One of the factors most carefully studied was the use of airplanes and bombing.

Before the end of the war, all airplanes and pilots had been taken from the control of the British Army and formed into a separate service—the Royal Air Force, or RAF. It was commanded by Major General Hugh Trenchard. Trenchard and two other generals who had been involved with air warfare, Italian Major General Giullo Douhet and the American Brigadier General Billy Mitchell, had similar ideas about the use of bombing. These men believed that future wars could be won by strategic bombing alone, and that land or sea battles might not even be necessary! They believed that nations would send huge fleets of long-range bombers against enemy cities day after

Major General Hugh Trenchard, known as the
"Father of the Royal Air Force"

day, destroying vital industries and shattering the morale of the enemy people, to force an end to the war. They also believed that while a nation had to use every possible means to defend itself against such a bombing campaign, the best defense would be to mount an even bigger bombing campaign against the enemy. In other words, they were insisting that a nation should depend almost entirely on air power to win wars.

These ideas became popular among British military leaders. After the war, at Trenchard's urging, the British began to build fleets of big long-range bombers. Aircraft manufacturers began trying to produce the fastest, most maneuverable, best-armed fighter plane possible. Weapon manufacturers worked to produce more effective anti-aircraft guns. Scientists were put to work to find methods of detecting the approach of enemy bombers before they arrived. Other countries also began similar programs.

In the years after World War I, people in most cities and large towns of Europe realized that if another war ever broke out, they would be the targets of large-scale air raids by fleets of bombers. This was made clear in 1936 and 1937, during the Spanish Civil War, when the cities of Madrid and Barcelona, as well as several small towns, were savagely bombed. The little town of Guernica was virtually destroyed by bombs, in an attempt to terrify people of other towns and cities into giving up.

Germany had been the loser in World War I, and the British Empire, France, and the other victors had imposed severe restrictions on it. Germany was not allowed to have an air force or navy, could not build any tanks, and had to keep its army small. Most German people bitterly resented this.

In 1933, the government of Germany was taken over by the Nazi political party. Their leader, Adolf Hitler, became head of the government and soon began efforts to make Germany a major military power again. Ignoring the restrictions, he increased the size of the German army, and began building a navy and an air force. The army was given a strong force of

Bomb damage in Guernica during the Spanish Civil War

excellent tanks and the world's first airborne divisions. The navy had fast, modern, powerful ships, and a menacing fleet of submarines. The German air force, the *Luftwaffe*, was soon regarded as the most powerful in the world, with large numbers of a deadly new weapon that no one else had, the dive-bomber. Fear that Germany might start another war began to spread through Europe.

War indeed broke out on September 1, 1939, when German armies swept across the border of Poland. The British and French declared war on Germany. This was the beginning of World War II.

The German tank divisions and dive bombers quickly and efficiently wiped out the Polish armies. Poland was conquered in less than a month. Several Polish cities were ruthlessly bombed, and this suggested what other cities of nations involved in the war could expect. Throughout Britain, France, and Germany, cities began to prepare for the terrible bombing raids that seemed certain. Anti-aircraft guns and searchlights were put in position. Underground bomb shelters, where people could seek safety during raids, were created in basements of large public buildings and sections of subways. Precious old and rare objects and paintings were taken out of museums and churches and stored in safe places, mainly underground. In Britain, some two million small children were evacuated from London and other large English cities, to foster homes in remote country towns, where they would be safe.

Cities began to have nightly blackouts. No streetlights, store or theater signs, or other outside lights were allowed on after sunset. Cars drove with their lights off. Windows of homes and apartments were covered with thick curtains. It was hoped that by keeping the city dark, bombers would be unable to locate their targets.

But no city was bombed, at first. British bombers droned over German cities, but dropped only propaganda messages urging Germany to make peace. Both sides seemed reluctant to begin mass bombings, a horror that could be launched against them in return.

However, the RAF bomber force, known as Bomber Command, attempted some raids against German warships in the port of Wilhelmshaven. They were made in broad daylight, and were a disaster. German fighter planes came swarming up, and on one day alone, half the 24 British bombers making the attack were shot down. This convinced those in charge of Bomber Command that all bombing raids should be made only at night.

In April 1940, Germany suddenly invaded Denmark and Norway, both neutral countries. A month later, Germany struck again, invading the Netherlands, Belgium, and France. The Dutch city of Rotterdam was ruthlessly bombed, its center gutted by fire; 980 people were killed, many more were injured, and some 78,000 were left homeless. This was deliberate terror bombing, and the Netherlands surrendered after only four days. Belgium was quickly conquered in only two more weeks.

France's army was thought to be the best in the world, and there was a small British army in France to help it, but the French and British were completely outclassed by the German *Blitzkrieg* ("lightning-war") tactics of tanks and dive-bombers, just as the Poles had been. A little less than eight weeks after the invasion began, France surrendered. The remains of the British army were evacuated from France by the British navy, in one of the greatest rescue operations in history.

Now Britain, the heart of the British Empire, stood alone. British military leaders felt sure that the might of the German army would soon be launched against Britain. This was precisely what Hitler and his generals were planning.

To invade Britain, German troops would have to cross the English Channel. They would be in constant danger from bombing by hundreds of British planes and gunfire from

Rotterdam on May 14, 1940: 980 people died and 78,000 lost their homes.

scores of British warships. The German air force could prevent this by attacking the British bombers with fighter planes and the British ships with bombers—but the British had fighter planes to protect their bombers and ships. So German commanders felt that for an invasion to be successful, the German air force would have to first destroy most of the RAF's Fighter Command, its force of fighter planes. This would give it air superiority—freedom to go after British bombers and ships with no interference.

The *Luftwaffe*'s commander, Reichsmarschall Hermann Goering, devised a plan to destroy the RAF Fighter Command. The *Luftwaffe* would begin continuous air attacks on Fighter Command airfields, to wipe out the existing British fighters as

Reichsmarschall Hermann Goering

quickly as possible. Meanwhile, factories that built fighter planes would be steadily bombed, to keep replacements from being produced. Eventually, the RAF would run out of fighter planes. When that happened, the invasion of Britain would begin!

Chapter 3

THE BATTLE OF BRITAIN

It seemed as if the *Luftwaffe* could easily carry out Goering's plan. It could put about 1,300 bombers and 900 fighters into the air. These were all propeller-driven; no jet aircraft existed yet.

The British had only about 640 fighters to oppose the *Luftwaffe*. However, the British had several undisclosed advantages.

For one, they had actually been preparing for air attacks for almost twenty years. They had produced a fighter plane called the Spitfire that was better than German fighters, with a speed of 370 miles (600 kilometers) an hour, the ability to turn very rapidly, and the firepower of eight machine guns. Another British fighter, the Hurricane, was slower than the German fighters, but more than a match for any of the bombers. The British planes would have an advantage in being close to their bases, whereas the Germans would be a long way from theirs.

Both the British and the Germans had developed radar, but British scientists had been able to make their radar far more

A British Supermarine Spitfire

Technicians at work repairing a British Hawker Hurricane

effective. Radar stations had been set up all along the English coast to detect planes coming across the channel; this would allow plenty of time for fighter-plane squadrons to get into the air and meet them. The Germans were unaware of this.

Most important of all, the British had deciphered the German air force's radio code. Simply by listening to the code messages broadcast, they would be able to tell exactly when air raids were being launched against them! The Germans were unaware of this, too.

The long series of German bombing attacks, known as the Battle of Britain, began on July 10, 1940. For several weeks,

German bombers, accompanied by fighter planes, mainly bombed ships in the waters off the coast, sinking a number. Their real purpose was to tempt British fighters to attack them. Fighters did come out, but from July 10 to August 12, the British shot down 286 German planes while losing only 150 of their own!

On August 15, the *Luftwaffe* sent out the largest number of planes yet used at one time in the war—432 bombers, 190 dive-bombers, and 975 fighters—in a determined effort to try to destroy many of the British airfields. Some airfields were damaged, but the fighters of the RAF shot down 75 German planes while losing only 34 of their own.

Unless the weather was bad, there were generally several attacks each day. For the British and German fliers the Battle of Britain became a day-to-day encounter with death. For German pilots, this meant a long flight over the Channel; for the British, it meant a rush to meet enemy planes as they entered the air above Britain. The two sides began vicious combat, the German bombers fighting to reach their target and drop their bombs, the German fighters trying to protect them so they could do so, and the British doing their utmost to destroy every bomber and eliminate any fighter that tried to stop them. For some twenty or thirty minutes, planes swooped, swerved, and dodged, and machine guns chattered. A wing or tail would be sliced off by bullets, so that a plane would fall whirling to the ground. A plane would burst into flame and plunge downward, leaving a trail of smoke. Bullets would tear into the bodies of fighter pilots and bomber crewmen, so that a plane might go into a screaming dive with its pilot dead or wounded and helpless, and smash into the ground.

Sometimes some bombers reached their target, sometimes none did. But German fighter planes could not carry enough fuel to stay over Britain for more than about thirty minutes. Then they would have to turn and head back across the

Channel. Generally, the British would pursue them for a distance; then they, too, would turn back and head for their home field. Usually, for both Germans and British, some planes—sometimes many—would not return.

At the airfields, ground crews quickly refueled the planes and rearmed their weapons. The pilots had a chance to eat something, to try to relax over a card game, or perhaps even to snatch a quick nap, while waiting for the next order to "scramble"—which might come in a few hours or less. Thus, the airmen on both sides often faced death several times a day.

The battle to destroy the RAF went on through August and into the first week of September. Through that period, the British actually destroyed more planes than they lost; 956 German to 550 British. But the British were in serious trouble. Their fighter force was shrinking, because they had lost more planes than the aircraft factories, most of which were damaged, were able to quickly replace. And their number of trained, skilled pilots was also shrinking, as men were killed and badly wounded in the daily combat. It was beginning to look as if the German plan to destroy the RAF's fighter force would be successful.

Then, something happened that changed everything.

What happened was a mistake. On the night of August 24, about a dozen German bombers accidentally overflew the targets they were supposed to hit and dropped their bombs in the middle of London. Houses were destroyed and people killed. It looked as if it was a deliberate terror bombing, such as the British had been fearing. Instantly, the British government decided Germany had to be punished. On the night of August 25, 81 British planes bombed the German capital city, Berlin.

The bombing did not do much damage, but it was a tremendous embarrassment to the *Luftwaffe* commander, Goering, who had once publicly stated that Berlin could never be bombed. Hitler was outraged by the British bombing, and he decided that Britain should be taught a lesson. He ordered the German air force to stop bombing airfields and factories and begin bombing British cities instead. Thus, the kind of bombing that had been feared from the beginning of the war, the bombing of cities to cause the greatest amount of death and destruction possible, began.

The first deliberate terror-bombing raid was made on London on September 7. About 320 bombers, accompanied by 648 fighter planes, came droning over the city. Docks and warehouses along the river were set afire, a huge ammunition factory was blown apart, and many blocks of homes were pulverized. That night, 250 more bombers attacked.

For the next week, London and other areas were hit with raids. People were warned of the approach of bombers by the sound of loud sirens. It was a mournful, howling sound that rose and fell, rose and fell. Hearing it, people rushed to the underground shelters or went to sheltered spots in their homes. When the raid was over, and the planes were definitely leaving, the sirens sounded again, but with an even, steady howl. This was known as the "all clear."

On September 15, the German air force made the largest attack ever sent against Britain. Some 400 bombers and 700 fighters, in various-sized groups, headed for London. A few flights got through, but most were broken up by British fighters and forced to drop their bombs wherever they could. The RAF lost 27 planes, but 56 German planes were shot down.

No one yet knew it, but this was a turning point. The German decision to switch from bombing airfields and factories to bombing cities had been a tremendous mistake that actually saved Britain from invasion, and helped it keep fighting the war. For it had given the British fighter plane squadrons the chance to rebuild their strength. They had come very close to being destroyed, but the attempt to destroy them had been sidetracked. The German air force had lost all

British prime minister Winston Churchill visits the aftermath of a German bombing raid on London.

chance of ever gaining air superiority, and the invasion of Britain was no longer possible. Two days later, Hitler "postponed" it, indefinitely.

The terror bombings continued through the rest of September and all of October. But there were fewer and fewer of them as time went on. By the end of October, the British knew the RAF had won the Battle of Britain! The German plan to destroy the RAF Fighter Command with air power had failed. The British had lost 915 planes, but Germany had lost 1,733. More than 23,000 people had been killed, many thousands more were injured, and factories and airports and cities had been damaged. But the German hope of an invasion that could win the war had melted away. The Battle of Britain, the major air battle of World War II, was over.

Chapter 4

BRITAIN STRIKES BACK

The battle to destroy the RAF Fighter Command was over, but the terror bombing of British cities was not. On November 14, in a ten-hour-long raid, 437 German bombers devastated the city of Coventry. They destroyed or damaged some 50,000 buildings, including the beautiful 700-year-old cathedral, and killed and injured more than 1,200 people. On December 29, 244 German bombers dropped many hundreds of incendiary bombs on the old medieval part of London, starting 1,500 fires.

Bad weather halted the bombing for a time, but it began again in February and went on into March and April. Cities in Northern Ireland and Scotland were hit, as well as English cities. The British called this period of steady city bombing "the Blitz," from the German word *Blitzkrieg*—lightning war.

But even as German bombers were pounding British cities, the RAF's Bomber Command was striking back. At first, only German military targets such as airfields and railroads were hit, but after Coventry was so ruthlessly bombed, British leaders again decided that Germany should be paid back. On the night

Coventry Cathedral lies in ruins after the Blitz.

of December 16, the German town of Mannheim was visited by 100 British bombers, and their crews deliberately aimed for houses, stores, and office buildings. This was a definite terror bombing, done as an act of vengeance.

For the first few months of 1941, Bomber Command made raids against German warships, on oil plants and railroads, and on several cities. Meanwhile, British military leaders tried to decide what the best use of Bomber Command would actually be.

Then, in June, Germany invaded the former Soviet Union. The German air raids on British cities now stopped, as the full force of the *Luftwaffe* was turned against the Soviets. So Great Britain now had an ally in the war against Hitler, and that helped bring a decision about the kind of bombing to do. British leaders decided the best way of helping its new ally would be to attack anything useful to Germany for getting troops and supplies into the Soviet Union—railroad yards, fuel-storage areas, munitions factories. Most of these were located in cities. A program of nighttime strategic bombing of special targets in certain German cities was ordered.

The main British bomber at this time was the Wellington Mark 1C, known by the nickname of "Wimpey," and these planes made most of the raids. The "Wimpey" was not a very large plane, and its interior was narrow and cramped. The front gunner had to reach his position in the plane's nose by crawling between the pilot's legs. The rear gunner had to walk bent double to get to his position at the tail. The men hung their parachutes on hooks and made themselves as comfortable as they could; the flight might take as long as eight hours going and returning. But it was impossible to be comfortable on such a flight. Even though the men were dressed in thick fleece-lined clothing, it was icy cold in the plane. Because of the altitude, the air was thin, and the men had to wear oxygen masks, which was unpleasant because every breath had a rubbery taste. The noise of the engines was ear-splitting, and the plane was constantly vibrating.

A Vickers Wellington Mark 1C bomber with a Spitfire escort

Because of the length of these flights, fighter planes, with their short ranges, could not go along to protect the bombers, and they were on their own. The German bombers that had attacked Britain had fairly short flights over the English Channel, and ran into anti-aircraft fire and fighter-plane attacks only when they reached the sky over Britain. But during much of their long flights to Germany, British bombers were in almost constant danger. Their course usually took them over German-occupied France, Belgium, or the Netherlands. As the coast came into view, the crews would be alerted by an announcement from the pilot. "Crossing enemy coast—NOW!" The men would grow tense. A fighter squadron might be waiting to pounce on them.

Even if there was no attack, there was always anti-aircraft fire. The gunners in their turrets and the pilot and copilot at the front of the plane saw sudden puffs of smoke appear, and the pilot quickly changed course to foil the gunners' aim.

In time the planes were over Germany, approaching the target city. Anti-aircraft shells bursting all around made each plane jounce and wobble. Fragments of exploding shells made little rips and tears in the fabric covering the planes' bodies, in the backs of seats, in the parachutes hanging from the hooks, and in the flesh of crewmen. Sometimes a burst was near enough to badly damage a plane. Sometimes a burst was directly on a plane, blowing it apart.

The bomb-bay doors in each plane's belly were opened, and after a moment the crew would hear the bombardier's voice—"Bombs gone!" Several miles below, explosions rocked the city as the bombs hit.

Searchlight beams slid all around the bombers, and German fighters were flashing through the sky. Cannon shells burst on wings, and bullets sliced through the bombers' bodies. Crewmen were hit, and killed or injured. Planes were burning, and parachutes blossomed in the sky as men bailed out, hoping to land safely. Planes were spiraling toward the ground with pilots dead at the controls.

Eventually, the surviving bombers of the flight left Germany, flying back over occupied territory. Again, they ran a course of anti-aircraft fire, and some were "jumped" by fighter planes. By the time they reached the Channel, another one or two might have gone down. Some were "limping" on one engine, with the other shot away or burning. Some had damaged wing flaps, shattered tail assemblies, or mangled landing gear that would make landing dangerous and difficult. Finally, the bombers would reach their field and land, one after another. Most would come down safely.

Weather permitting, the bomber crews would go through this ordeal every night for a number of days, have a few days off, and then do it again.

After a time, the generals in charge of Bomber Command became aware that their nightly bombing raids were not very effective. Aerial photographs taken after raids and information supplied by spies in Germany revealed that far less damage was being done than the bomber crews believed they were doing. Targets were being only partly hit, and many were even missed altogether. Sometimes even the wrong places were being bombed!

Simply finding the way to a particular place through several hundred miles of darkness was terribly difficult. Navigators, whose job was to find the way to the target, had little to work with except maps and compasses. There were no computers at that time, and no instruments or devices to help with navigation. Unless there was strong moonlight it was very difficult to see anything, and even a large city with all its lights off could easily be missed. Picking out a small target, such as a factory or particular building, from several miles above a darkened city was almost impossible.

Making matters worse, the bomber forces were beginning to take serious losses due to improved German radar. British bombers sent to hit targets in the Ruhr area of Germany were losing almost one-quarter of their force each time. If this continued, Bomber Command would soon hardly have enough planes to make any raids!

The head of the British government, Prime Minister Winston Churchill, and his military leaders considered the problems of bombing. They determined that strategic bombing—the bombing of special targets such as factories and rail centers—simply wasn't accurate enough to have much effect on the German war effort, and might as well be given up. In November 1941, Churchill ordered Bomber Command to suspend attacks on Germany for a time, and build up strength for a renewed effort in the coming year.

Then something happened that altered the entire direction of the war. The United States, with its enormous manpower and its tremendous ability to produce everything from dozens of battleships to thousands of bombers, entered the war on the British side.

Chapter 5

AMERICA JOINS IN

On December 7, 1941, the United States was violently pulled into the war. Hundreds of planes from aircraft carriers of the Japanese Imperial Navy made a surprise attack on the American naval base at Pearl Harbor, Hawaii. This was a strategic raid against American warships in the harbor, and it was a huge success. Three battleships were sunk, five seriously damaged, and a number of other ships sunk and damaged. The United States declared war on the Empire of Japan. Four days later, Germany and Italy, which were allies of Japan, declared war on the United States.

Japan had also gone to war against the British Empire. American and British leaders had already met and agreed that Germany was a greater threat than Japan, so they would just try to hold Japan in check while working to beat Germany as quickly as possible. When the two European powers were defeated, the United States and Great Britain would turn their military might on Japan.

Clouds of smoke pour from the USS Arizona *after Japanese bombers hit it in the attack on Pearl Harbor.*

A number of American military and naval officers were quickly sent to Britain to set up procedures for the American armed forces to work with the British armed forces. Some of these officers were members of the U.S. Army Air Force, and in January 1942, they began putting together the main organization for American air operations in Europe—the United States Eighth Air Force.

In February, the British High Command decided that the only kind of bombing that could actually do harm to the German war effort was the steady, deliberate bombing of major industrial cities. Every bomb dropped on a city was bound to damage something, whether a factory making weapons, a warehouse full of supplies, or a family's home. If enough bombs were dropped, both the city's ability to produce war materials and the will of its citizens to keep the war going could be destroyed. Thus, the RAF Bomber Command was ordered to embark on a gigantic continuous program of bombing German cities.

On the night of March 28, the RAF Bomber Command began the first of these raids. The German port city of Lübeck became the target of 234 bombers. The British had developed some new ideas to increase the effectiveness of their air raids, and now they tried them. Some of the bombers were equipped with a new navigation device that helped them find the target more easily. These planes went in first and dropped flares and incendiary bombs that lit up the city with fires. The rest of the bombers simply headed for the glow of the fires and dropped their bombs when they were overhead. The raid was devastating. Half the city was virtually destroyed.

Americans were heartened that one of their enemies, at least, was taking some punishment. But America had done very little against Japan. There was no chance for any raids to be made on Japanese cities, for the closest American base to Japan was more than 2,000 miles (3,220 kilometers) away, much too far for any American bomber to get to Japan and return.

The cathedral in Lübeck in flames after an Allied air raid

Yet in April, 1942, Americans learned that U.S. bombers *had* bombed cities in Japan! On April 18, sixteen U.S. B-25s bombed the Japanese capital, Tokyo, and several other major cities. These bombings did not really cause much destruction, but they shocked the Japanese people, who had been assured Japan could never be bombed, and puzzled Japanese military leaders, who couldn't figure out where the bombers had come from.

The origin was an example of American inventiveness. The planes that had bombed Japan were North American B-25B Mitchell Mark 1's. This plane needed a long stretch of ground to take off, but sixteen B-25 crews, under the leadership of

Lieutenant Colonel James H. "Jimmie" Doolittle, an American hero of World War I, had rigorously trained to take off from the deck of an aircraft carrier. (This would have seemed impossible to most aircraft experts.) The U.S. carrier *Hornet*, with sixteen planes aboard, sailed to within 650 miles (1,050 kilometers) of Japan, well within the bombers' range, and the B-25s took off from the ship and made the raid.

It was a one-way operation, however. B-25s could take off from a carrier deck, but they couldn't land on one. So arrangements had been made for the bombers to land in China, an American ally. Most of them made it there, and one landed in the Soviet Union.

The "Doolittle Raid," as it was called, gave Americans a terrific boost in morale. But things were still going badly for America and its allies in the Pacific. Then, in June, a stunning American victory in the naval Battle of Midway suddenly turned the tide, putting Japan on the defensive. The United States began to launch a series of invasions of Japanese island-bases in the Pacific, moving ever closer toward the heart of the Japanese Empire.

In Britain, work was progressing on the many airfields needed for the American Eighth Air Force, and the Eighth's Bomber Command was beginning to get its weapons, big four-engine Boeing B-17E bombers. This plane was known as the "Flying Fortress," because it bristled with machine guns.

But there was disagreement between the British and American airmen. The British were convinced that night bombing was the only way to conduct air raids in order to keep from losing too many planes and also to cause the most destruction and chaos. They believed that if the Americans would join them in making nighttime raids on Germany, it would bring the war to a quick end.

The Americans believed just as firmly that only daylight raids, when pilots could clearly see the targets, could do any real

A B-25 Mitchell Mark I takes off from the USS Hornet *on its way to bomb Tokyo, Japan.*

damage. To keep their plane losses down, they had developed a special technique for daylight bombing. They would come over the target at a very high altitude, making it harder for anti-aircraft fire to hit them. They would fly in a tight, close-together formation, so the planes could protect each other with their machine guns, making it hard for fighters to attack them.

Boeing B-17Es—"Flying Fortresses"—on a daylight raid of a German fighter base. The black smoke below and behind the central bomber is anti-aircraft fire.

Eighth Air Force bombers made their first raid on September 17. In daylight, twelve B-17s droned over the German-held city of Rouen, France, and bombed a major railroad center that the Germans needed for sending troops and supplies all over France. It was severely damaged, and no bombers were lost. It looked as if daylight bombing was quite practical.

Meanwhile, the RAF Bomber Command was looking for more ways to make night bombing more efficient, and in August it created what was known as the Pathfinder Force. These were groups of bombers that would head toward a target, dropping a steady string of flares on parachutes. They floated slowly down, providing a trail of light for the main force of bombers to follow straight to the target.

The Americans continued to make small raids on targets in France for a few months. The RAF Bomber Command continued its night raids on German targets. Then, on November 8, an American and British army commanded by U.S. General Dwight Eisenhower invaded North Africa. This army helped defeat German and Italian troops fighting a British army in North Africa, and North Africa became an Allied base.

In January 1943, Allied leaders met to decide the direction of the war. One of the things they determined to do was to intensify the strategic bombing of German cities. They agreed to begin a campaign of bombing Germany around the clock, with the American Eighth Air Force making raids during the day, while the RAF Bomber Command made them at night. Bombing the already shattered German cities was now to be virtually doubled.

Chapter 6

LOST BOMBERS, BLASTED CITIES

The new bombing offensive against Germany was code-named "Operation Pointblank." Bomber Command's mission was to completely destroy the everyday life of German cities, by demolishing homes, workplaces, and transportation. The Americans would strike mainly at German industry, particularly airplane factories.

On January 27, the Eighth Air Force made its first daylight raid on Germany. The Eighth had been equipped with some new bombers, Consolidated B-24 Liberators, and 27 B-24s and 64 B-17s made the raid. Many planes were forced to turn back by bad weather, but 53 managed to reach Wilhelmshaven and drop their bombs on a submarine factory. Fighting off attacks by German fighters, they headed for home, losing only one plane and crew. The bombing seemed to show, again, that daylight raids could be made without losing a lot of planes. However, when another raid was made on Wilhelmshaven in February, seven bombers were shot down.

A de Havilland Mosquito plane

The center of Essen reduced to rubble by bombing raids

By night, planes of the RAF Bomber Command pounded German cities. On March 5th, the British began a series of raids that became known as "Battles," starting with the Battle of the Ruhr, the great industrial region of western Germany. The first target was the city of Essen, home of the Krupp Works, a giant industrial firm that produced weapons and munitions. Four hundred forty-two bombers roared over the city, and with them was something new—eight de Havilland Mosquito fighter-bombers equipped with "Oboe," a device that enabled the planes to locate their targets by means of radar. The Mosquitoes headed straight for the Krupp factories and dropped target-indicator bombs, which exploded at a certain height in a shower of slow-burning red or yellow flares. Twenty-two Pathfinder bombers followed them and dropped green flares over the area. The remaining hundreds of bombers simply flew toward these "Christmas-tree lights" and dropped their bombs. The Krupp factories were severely damaged, and 160 acres (65 hectares) of Essen turned into rubble. Fourteen bombers were shot down.

For nearly four months, Essen and other Ruhr cities were hammered. Cities were not the only targets. The night of May 16, 19 British bombers attacked several dams on two rivers in the Ruhr valley. Two dams were blown open and a third damaged; 334 tons of water burst out, flooding a large area. Electric power was knocked out, areas of railroad track were under water, bridges were washed away, factories were flooded out—and thousands of people, asleep in their homes, were drowned. Eight bombers and 56 crewmen were lost.

Next came the Battle of Hamburg. Hamburg was Germany's third-largest city, an important northern seaport. The night of July 24, 791 British bombers carrying 2,460 tons of high-explosive and incendiary bombs struck the city. They were also equipped with a new weapon known as "window," to disrupt and confuse German radar. It consisted of millions of strips of aluminum tape, much like Christmas-tree tinsel. Dumped out of each bomber, masses of it floated slowly to the ground. On German radar screens, it suddenly seemed as if there were thousands of British bombers, making it impossible for anti-aircraft guns and searchlights, which were guided by radar, to know where to look or where to shoot. Searchlight beams desperately stabbed back and forth, and anti-aircraft gun crews began firing blindly, hoping to hit something by luck. Fighter planes headed for what looked like bombers on their radar, only to find themselves attacking clouds of "window."

Flying over the city in almost complete safety, the British unloaded their bombs, explosive bombs first, then many thousands of incendiaries. Almost every one started a fire.

The next day, 109 American Eighth Air Force B-17s came over Hamburg, which lay under a thick blanket of black smoke from many fires. The Americans bombed the dock and harbor area and some factories.

The night of July 27, 279 British bombers struck the city again. They dropped mostly incendiary bombs. The fires grew and spread. For the first time a "firestorm" occurred. So many huge fires were burning close together among tall buildings that the air over the city became superheated. This created a tornado-like effect, pulling the incredibly hot air into the burning area, setting everything ablaze and making the fire spread out as fast as a person might run. This wave of fire swept an area some 4 square miles (10 square kilometers) in size. The temperature was so high the asphalt streets melted, and people in underground shelters were incinerated into fine ash!

When the four days of bombing were finished, 48,000 people were dead, many thousands were hurt, 455,000 homes had been destroyed or badly damaged, and the wrecks of 55 ships lay in the harbor. The city was in ruins. Bomber Command had lost 87 planes, but regarded the Battle of Hamburg as a tremendous victory.

Top American air force generals had decided that strikes should be made against Germany's sources of fuel oil for its planes and tanks. The best target seemed to be the vast Ploesti oil fields in Rumania, which was under German control. A damaging raid on Ploesti could be a serious blow to Germany's fuel supply. Bombers couldn't reach Ploesti from Britain, but by taking off from airfields in North Africa, with extra fuel tanks, they could get there and back. On August 1, 124 Eighth Air Force B-24s joined 54 B-24s of the U.S. Ninth Air Force, which had been formed in North Africa in 1942, and set out to hammer Ploesti.

Hamburg after air raids

Ploesti, however, was heavily defended, and the bombers, flying at low altitudes to avoid radar, ran into a storm of anti-aircraft fire and were jumped by fighters. Fifty-three Liberators were shot down, 55 others so badly damaged that many had to be scrapped. These were enormous losses, and the raid did not affect Ploesti's output of oil.

On August 17, Eighth Air Force bombers attempted their farthest raid into Germany yet, to bomb important factories in the northern cities of Schweinfurt and Regensburg. They found 300 *Luftwaffe* fighters waiting for them!

The *Luftwaffe* pilots had worked out new defense tactics against daylight bombing. Many German planes had been equipped with devices for firing rockets, which could destroy a bomber with a single explosion. Other fighters had been outfitted to drop bombs, and they flew above the American bombers and actually dropped bombs on them! Sixty bombers were destroyed or shot down, and 47 damaged. These, too, were extremely high losses. Eighth Air Force commanders decided to hold off on any more long-range raids for a time.

August 17 was also the day of a special mission for the RAF Bomber Command. Allied agents had discovered the Germans were constructing two new kinds of secret weapons. One was a giant rocket-propelled explosive missile, the other, a robot-controlled airplane that was a flying bomb. These were being constructed on the tiny island of Peenemünde, off the north coast of Germany. Bomber Command was given the order to make an all-out attack on the island.

The head of Bomber Command, Air Marshal Arthur Harris, put his entire force of 596 planes into the raid. But he sent eight Mosquito bombers to Berlin, to drop flares as if a raid were about to be made there. This trick worked, and most of the German fighters guarding Peenemünde hurried to Berlin. The British bombers swept over Peenemünde, dropping 2,000 tons of bombs. They shattered buildings and killed some of the important scientists working on the secret project. It was set back for weeks, but not destroyed.

In September, American and British armies invaded Italy. Italy surrendered and dropped out of the war. But German forces in Italy continued to put up a determined, vicious fight. A new American Air Force, the Fifteenth, was set up in Italy.

As autumn arrived, the Eighth Air Force decided to make another try against the city of Schweinfurt. On October 14, 291 fortresses were sent. The result was a disaster that became known as "Black Thursday" to the men of the Eighth Air Force. Although the Schweinfurt factories were badly damaged,

Lancaster bombers during an attack on the German island Wangerooge

another 60 American bombers were shot down and 138 seriously damaged, some enough to be scrapped. These losses were so severe that the Eighth Air Force actually had to drop out of Operation Pointblank for a while, until the planes—and crews—could be replaced.

Air Marshal Harris had wanted American help for a plan he had, but now was forced to go ahead without it. Harris still believed firmly that wars could be won with giant bombing raids that literally destroyed cities. On November 18, 444 RAF Bomber Command Lancasters began the Battle of Berlin, with the first of 16 giant night raids on the German capital. Harris intended to bomb Berlin into ruins to end the war!

Chapter 7

THE LAST DAYS OF GERMANY

As 1944 began, Berlin had been bombed seven times and parts of it were in ruins, but the war was still going on. German armies were fighting hard and well in both the Soviet Union and against British and American forces in Italy. German industry was still producing plenty of materials for the war. Most German people still wanted their country to fight on. Thus, the bombings of Berlin had not accomplished what Harris expected. Furthermore, the RAF Bomber Command was taking terrible losses for the bombings. The *Luftwaffe* fighter force was still strong, and it was making Bomber Command pay for the damage to German cities and deaths of German people.

The Allied armies were to invade France in 1944; the invasion was to take place in June. But just as the German commanders in 1940 had known they had to destroy the RAF's fighter force before trying to invade Britain, Allied commanders now knew the German fighter force had to be destroyed or the Allied invasion might fail. American air force commanders

Allied bombing of Berlin decimated the city.

in Europe put together a plan to eliminate the German fighters. They intended to send hordes of fighter planes to shoot the German fighters out of the sky, and hordes of bombers to bomb the airfields where they were kept, the oil refineries that produced their fuel, and the factories that built new planes to replace those lost. This plan, which was much like Reichs- marschall Goering's 1940 plan, was code-named Operation Argument.

Operation Argument was assigned to the U.S. Eighth and Fifteenth Air Forces. It was launched on February 20, when nearly one thousand Eighth Air Force bombers set out to smash aircraft factories in several German cities. With them was a new weapon—long-range fighter planes that could stay with the bombers all the way to the target and protect them from the German fighters.

While the Americans were trying to wipe out the *Luftwaffe* fighters with "Argument," the RAF Bomber Command, with some American help, was still fighting the Battle of Berlin. By the end of March, Berlin had been bombed sixteen times, by British bombers at night and American bombers by day. Many other cities were also hit repeatedly. But Air Marshal Harris's plan had failed. Berlin was in almost total ruin, but Germany was still fighting, and the RAF Bomber Command had taken shattering losses. In the bombings of Berlin and the other cities, 1,047 British bombers had been shot down or destroyed, and 1,682 badly damaged. The Battle of Berlin was a victory for Germany, a defeat for the RAF Bomber Command.

But as time went on, it became clear that Operation Argument was working. The American fighter planes were taking a toll, and the *Luftwaffe* Fighter Command was in serious trouble. Germany's most skilled, experienced pilots were being killed and wounded at an ever-increasing rate, and there were no replacements for them. Although German industry was still producing plenty of fighter planes, the *Luftwaffe* was running out of men to fly them. Thus, fewer and fewer German fighters were appearing in the sky. By the beginning of June, the Allies had done what Germany was unable to do in 1940—they had achieved air superiority!

On June 15, the greatest invasion in all history began. Brought to the northern coast of France by thousands of ships, British and American armies landed on French soil and fought to push German forces out of the country and back into Germany. Nearly ten thousand Allied bombers and fighter planes filled the air above them. Almost no German planes were seen in the sky.

The German forces in France were slowly driven back, and by the beginning of winter they had been pushed to the German border. But they were still fighting, hard and skillfully. In the Netherlands they defeated a massive attack by Allied airborne troops, and in Belgium they started a smashing attack of their own, the Battle of the Bulge. The war was far from over.

Air Marshal Harris and some other military leaders urged combining the British and American bomber forces in one more immense bombing campaign to destroy several German cities in hope of finally breaking the spirit of the German people and ending the war. This idea was finally agreed on. The code-name for the campaign was Operation Thunderclap. The cities to be bombed were Berlin, Leipzig, Chemnitz, and Dresden.

Dresden was one of the most beautiful old cities of Europe. It had not been hit much by Allied bombing, so it was still in good condition. There was really no good reason for it to be bombed. It had almost no factories, so it was not really of much importance to the German war effort. But, for reasons that are still open to debate, it was picked as the main target for Operation Thunderclap.

On the night of February 13, 234 British Lancaster bombers flew over Dresden at nine o'clock, fanning out as they

The firebombing of Dresden was devastating.

came. Three hours later, a flight of 538 Lancasters droned over the city. At about noon the next day, 311 American Flying Fortresses made a bombing run. Dresden was undefended. There was no anti-aircraft fire, and no German fighter planes appeared during any of these raids.

Three-fourths of the more than 3,000 tons of bombs that were dropped were incendiaries. As happened in Hamburg, a firestorm erupted. The city of Dresden burned for a week. About 80,000 homes were completely destroyed and 250,000 people left homeless. Most of Dresden's treasured old medieval buildings, churches, and palaces were destroyed or horribly damaged. It is not known how many people were actually killed. The official record says at least 35,000, but it may really have been as many as 100,000. Dresden had been devastated!

A few more attacks were made on several cities, but on April 16, 1945, the British-American air offensive against Germany was officially ended. The cities of Germany were in ruins. Allied armies were pushing into Germany from the west, Soviet armies from the east. On May 7, Germany surrendered.

Operation Pointblank had cost the lives of 79,265 American and 79,281 British airmen. It is not known how many German airmen were killed, but about 305,000 German civilians died in the bombings, and many thousands were injured. Beautiful old cities, with buildings that had stood for hundreds of years, had been pulverized into rubble. But it was not the ruin of its cities that forced Germany to surrender. Germany surrendered only when its army no longer had equipment and supplies to continue to fight with.

Chapter 8

THE BOMBING OF JAPAN

While European cities were being smashed by bombs, the cities of America and Japan remained unharmed. But in the spring of 1944, the U.S. Twentieth Air Force was created for a special purpose—to be the air force responsible for bombing the cities of Japan in order to end the war in the Pacific.

By November 1944, the United States had captured enough bases sufficiently close to Japan that American bombers could make raids from them anywhere on the Japanese islands. A program of air raids on Japanese aircraft factories began to wipe out Japan's production of fighter planes. This was the first step toward destroying Japan's ability to defend itself.

The Boeing B-29 Superfortress was the main American bomber. With them the Twentieth Air Force began the steady bombing of Japan in mid-November of 1944. As the Eighth Air Force had been doing in Europe, the bombers flew in tight formations, usually at a high altitude of 30,000 feet—a little less than 6 miles (10 kilometers). Although they took off from Pacific islands where the temperature was generally quite hot,

B-29 Superfortresses on a raid on Japan

the air 6 miles up was as bitterly cold and thin as in Europe, and the airmen had to wear warm heavy clothing, fur-lined boots, and oxygen masks, just as airmen in Europe did. High as the planes were, they were still in range of Japanese anti-aircraft guns and of some Japanese fighter planes. Many of these were flown by young pilots who did their best to simply smash into a bomber, perfectly willing to kill themselves if they could bring down an enemy plane.

By January 1945, it was obvious that high-level bombing wasn't effective. A new commander, General Curtis LeMay, was put in charge of bombing operations. By March, LeMay decided that high-level bombing would never work. The Twentieth Air Force was having the same problem that the RAF Bomber Command had in 1941—not enough bombs were hitting factories and other targets to do any real damage. In three months, 22 high-level raids had been made but only one aircraft factory knocked out. Yet at the same time, 102 B-29s had been lost. The damage to factories was nowhere near enough to justify such a loss of planes and airmen.

Japan's factory production had to be destroyed by other means, and LeMay thought he had the solution. Most factories and other targets were on the outskirts of cities of thousands of houses, where the factory workers lived. Most houses were built of wood, and the inside walls forming the rooms were actually made of paper. Fire would quickly and widely spread among such houses. LeMay felt sure that raids by hundreds of bombers dropping hundreds of incendiary bombs would burn up much of a Japanese city. He believed, as British Air Marshal Harris had believed about the Battle of Berlin, that such destruction would crush the will of the Japanese people to keep on fighting. He made the decision to firebomb the cities of Japan.

Tokyo was the first objective, serving as a test, to set a pattern for others. On the night of March 9, 279 B-29s swept over Tokyo in groups of three at a low altitude that surprised the

Japanese anti-aircraft gunners, who were prepared for a much higher target. Two kinds of incendiary bombs were used. One was a metal cylinder filled with 100 pounds (45 kilograms) of napalm, a jellied gasoline. When the cylinder hit, the napalm burst into flame and stuck to whatever it hit. Each plane in the first three squadrons carried 184 of these bombs, and every bomb started a fire. The fires guided the rest of the squadrons to the target area. Those planes carried 1,600 6-pound (3-kilogram) incendiaries, in clusters of 40. A cluster was dropped every 50 feet (15 meters), separating into 40 bombs that fell onto an area of about one-fourth of a square mile. The sky rained fire bombs!

Unluckily for the citizens of Tokyo, an extremely strong wind was blowing over the city. Fires began to spread and join, fanned by the wind into a raging firestorm that roared through nearly 16 square miles. This area became so hot that the water in the canals running through it actually boiled! 276,791 homes were turned to ashes. Some 83,000 people were killed, nearly 41,000 more injured, and more than a million left homeless. Fourteen bombers were shot down by anti-aircraft fire.

The firebombing of Tokyo was the most destructive air raid in history at that time. General LeMay decided it had been a success. He ordered the firebombings of other Japanese cities.

On March 11, the big industrial city of Nagoya was hit. On March 13, the port city of Osaka was turned into a sea of flame. On March 16 the city of Kobe was attacked. These raids killed and injured tens of thousands, destroyed hundreds of thousands of homes, and left millions homeless.

The raids went on and on. Other cities were hit, and cities that had already been bombed were bombed again. By the middle of 1945, Japan was in desperate condition. Its navy had virtually been destroyed, and its air force was reduced to almost nothing. Its major cities were burned-out ruins. Most Japanese people realized that Japan had lost the war.

Tokyo after firebombing

However, Japanese military leaders had no thought of surrendering. American military leaders grimly began to consider
that it might be necessary to invade and conquer Japan to end
the war. But Japanese soldiers had shown they would fight to the
death rather than give up. American leaders feared that an invasion of Japan could cost as much as a million American dead,
and even more Japanese.

But America had developed a secret weapon, the atomic
bomb. An exploding atomic bomb became a virtual tiny sun,

Hiroshima, August 6, 1945

pouring out a sledgehammer blast of incredible heat and deadly radiation. U.S. President Harry Truman and his advisers decided to use the atomic bomb as a threat to force Japan to surrender.

On July 26, the United States sent a message to the Japanese government describing the atomic bomb's power and urging surrender. There was no reply, and it was obvious the Japanese did not intend to surrender—they were preparing a massive defense against invasion. So, on August 6, three B-29s flew over the Japanese city of Hiroshima, and one dropped an atomic bomb. Hiroshima was essentially destroyed, 140,000 people were left dead and dying.

Radio broadcasts and newspaper stories throughout America announced the dropping of the atomic bomb. The bomb was generally described as ten times more powerful than the biggest bombs then being used. It was predicted that Japan would have to surrender in the face of such a powerful weapon. Nearly everyone in the country, and American servicemen around the world, were overjoyed to know that America had such a weapon and to think that, because of it, the war might soon end. No one objected to using it. It was regarded simply as a new kind of weapon, a more powerful and effective bomb than any other kind.

Once more, the U.S. sent a message to Japan, warning that another atomic bomb would be dropped if surrender was not quickly made. Again, there was no reply. Thus, on August 9, a second bomb was dropped on the city of Nagasaki. According to Japanese records, 73,774 people were killed.

On August 15, the Japanese Emperor made an announcement by radio. He told the Japanese people that Japan had no choice but to stop fighting. So World War II was over. However, it was probably neither the firebombing nor the atomic bombs that forced the surrender. It seems certain the Japanese army and Japanese people would have kept on fighting despite them. Japan surrendered only because the Emperor ordered it to.

From the beginning of the twentieth century, the bombing of cities and civilians was established as a major part of warfare. The men who flew the bombers in World Wars I and II were members of the military who were obeying orders with tremendous bravery. But perhaps it was the ordinary people who lived through the bombings who showed the greatest courage of all.

Ground Zero (where the bomb hit), Nagasaki, before and after

Index